12-17

THE AMAZING HUMAN BODY

Growth and Aging

Edited by
Joanne Randolph

Enslow Publishing
101 W. 23rd Street
Suite 240
New York, NY 10011
USA

enslow.com

This edition published in 2018 by:
Enslow Publishing, LLC.
101 W. 23rd Street, Suite 240
New York, NY 10011

Library of Congress Cataloging-in-Publication Date

Names: Randolph, Joanne, editor.
Title: Growth and aging / edited by Joanne Randolph.
Description: New York, NY : Enslow Publishing, 2018. | Series: The amazing human body | Audience: Grades 5-8. |
  Includes bibliographical references and index.
Identifiers: LCCN 2017001987| ISBN 9780766089839 (library-bound) | ISBN 9780766089815 (pbk.) | ISBN
  9780766089822 (6-pack)
Subjects: LCSH: Growth—Juvenile literature. | Aging—Juvenile literature.
Classification: LCC QH511 .G72 2018 | DDC 612.6/7—dc23
LC record available at https://lccn.loc.gov/2017001987

Printed in China

To Our Readers: We have done our best to make sure all website addresses in this book were active and appropriate when we went to press. However, the author and the publisher have no control over and assume no liability for the material available on those websites or on any websites they may link to. Any comments or suggestions can be sent by email to customerservice@enslow.com.

Photos Credits: Cover, p. 1 MJTH/Shutterstock.com; ksenia_bravo/Shutterstock.com (series logo); p. 3, back cover Tusiy/Shutterstock.com; pp. 4, 10, 18, 22, 30, 36 vitstudio/Shutterstock.com (DNA art), SUWIT NGAOKAEW/Shutterstock.com (chemical structure background); p. 5 Apple Tree House/Iconica/Getty Images; p. 7 Tim Vernon/Science Photo Library/Getty Images; p. 11 Jakub Krechowicz/Getty Images; p. 13 Michael Steele/Getty Images; p. 15 Yiu Yu Hoi/DigitalVision/Getty Images; p. 16 Stephen Dalton/Minden Pictures/Getty Images; p. 19 Gwen Shockey/Science Source; p. 20 Radius Images/Getty Images; p. 23 laflor/E+/Getty Images; pp. 24, 27 Designua/Shutterstock.com; p. 29 De Agostini Picture Library/Getty Images; p. 32 Monkey Business Images/Shutterstock.com; p. 34 bikeriderlondon/Shutterstock.com; p. 35 Manuel Litran/Paris Match Archive/Getty Images; p. 38 Science Source; p. 39 Boston Globe/Getty Images; p. 41 Kerdkanno/Shutterstock.com; p. 42 Jacek Chabraszewski/Shutterstock.com.

Article Credits: Glenn Murphy, "Growing Pains," *Ask*; Ilima Loomis "Even Steven," *Muse*; Alison Palmer, "Uniquely Identical," *Odyssey*; Faith Hickman Brynie, "The Telltale Tails of Telomeres," *Odyssey*; Margaret A. Hill, "Human Life Span: What Are the Limits?" *Odyssey*; Kathiann M. Kowalski, "Mind vs. Time: What's Ahead for the Aging Brain?" *Odyssey*.

CONTENTS

CHAPTER 1

GROWING PAINS

Why do our bodies grow the way they do, and how do they know when to stop? The tiny egg cell you grew from was smaller than the head of a pin. By the time you are fully grown, your body will be up to twenty thousand times larger. That's a lot of growing!

People grow at different rates. Growth rate depends on a person's genes, nutrition, and other factors.

HOW DO WE GROW?

In all animals—humans included—growth happens as cells swell, divide, and connect up. Even after you reach your full height, new cells are always growing to replace old ones, which are lost or recycled by the thousands every day.

Growth happens all over your body, and different body parts grow at different speeds. By the time you're ten years old, your head is almost adult size, but the rest of you may take another ten years to catch up! Inside your body, your heart, lungs, liver, and other organs all grow at their own rates. Your height comes mostly from how your bones grow.

As your spine and the long bones in your legs and arms get longer, you get taller. But this stretching and lengthening is far from steady—it speeds up during two super-speedy growth spurts, the first when you are a baby, and the second when you are a teenager. In just your first year of life, you grew about 10 inches (25 centimeters)! After that, your growth slowed down to about 1 to 3 inches (3 to 8 centimeters) each year. When you reach puberty, you may shoot up by 4 inches (10 centimeters) a year or more.

NOW, STOP!

But at some point, your body has to stop getting bigger. You might secretly wish you were 10 feet (3 meters) tall—but that's not likely to happen. Like other animals, human beings have evolved to be just the right size. We keep growing until we're large enough to survive alone and unprotected. If we're too small, we can't defend ourselves. But if we grow too large, it puts a dangerous strain on our bones, joints, and hearts.

Exactly how big any animal, including you, will get is coded into its deoxyribonucleic acid, or DNA. Your DNA is like a very long recipe for making you. There is a complete copy inside every cell. Cells follow different parts of the DNA instructions based on where the cell is in your body and chemical signals from other cells. DNA tells each cell what to be (say, a liver cell or a bone cell) and whether it should keep dividing, or stop.

Chemical messengers called hormones trigger much of your growth. Hormones are made in special glands and flow through

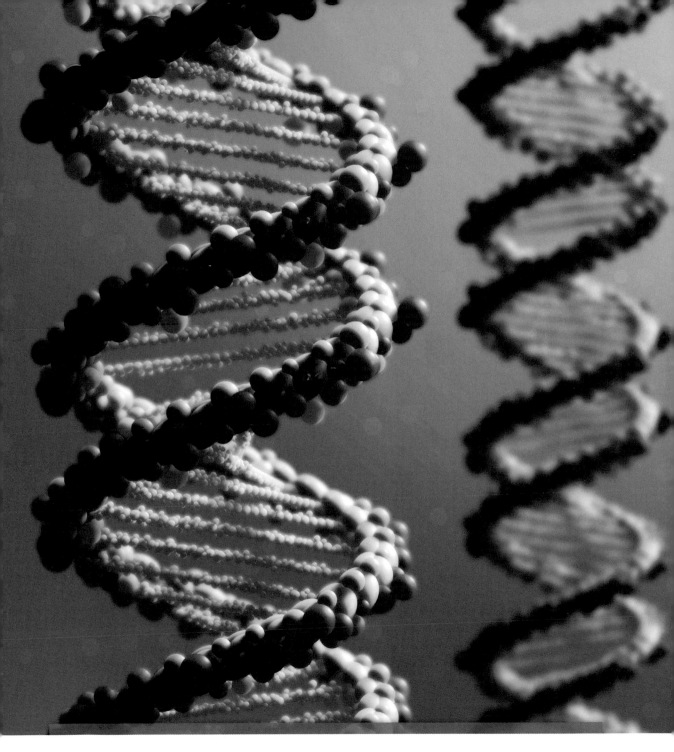

DNA, the blueprint of life, has two strands that are connected
by hydrogen bonds. It has a double-helix shape.

your bloodstream, relaying messages to cells. Your body makes different amounts of hormones at different stages in your life. As a baby and during puberty, they flood your blood. Girls usually get their growth spurts earlier—so for a couple of years at school, girls are taller than boys.

Once you've gone through puberty, you're fully developed. You've grown big and strong enough to survive without your parents, and eventually, to raise a family of your own. So the purpose of growing is complete. Your body makes fewer hormones, your cells get the message to stop dividing so quickly, and you stop getting bigger. You've grown up!

HOW TALL WILL YOU BE?

That depends on the genes (sections of DNA) you inherit from your mom and dad. Most children end up roughly as tall as their parents, or somewhere in between. Sometimes children grow taller than their parents, if their growth signals are more active and tell their bones to keep growing for a longer time. In rare cases, errors (like typos) in the DNA can cause the body to make too little or too much growth hormone, and the body may stop growing too soon, or keep growing too long.

Your cells are working hard to grow you toward your proper height. But to get there your body also needs the right building materials: healthy food, sleep, exercise, and sunshine (to make vitamin D, for strong bones). So, if you want to grow big and strong, don't bother stretching your legs every day, or sleeping upside down like a bat—just eat right, go out and play, and leave the rest to your DNA.

GROWTH IS SWELL

In a way, your body never stops growing. Growth happens inside living bodies as cells swell up, separate, and form networks of tissues and organs. Even when you stop getting larger, your body keeps growing throughout your life as worn-out cells die and new ones replace them. Your skin, muscles, blood, bones, even your brain— your whole body regenerates (or re-grows) itself nonstop. Every seven to ten years, your body will replace every cell. So, in a sense, you're not the same person you were even a few years ago!

GROWING BONES

Bones are built by special bone-building cells called osteoblasts. These cells send out a net of stringy collagen fibers (the tough, gristly bits that are hard to chew on chicken legs are made of these). These nets trap chalky calcium chunks to form hard, brittle bone. Once the osteoblasts are surrounded by trapped calcium, they become spiky osteocytes. Long bones like your thigh bone (or femur) have patches of these cells at each end, called growth plates, that lengthen the bone in both directions. They begin doing this at birth and continue until you reach your full adult height.

Chapter 2

Even Steven

More than five hundred years ago, the artist and scientist Leonardo da Vinci made a sketch of what was considered at the time to be the ideal human body. His famous drawing of the "Vitruvian Man" shows a handsome man of perfect proportions, each outstretched arm and leg exactly the same length as its mate.

The illustration offers an example of bilateral symmetry—where the left and right side of a body are more or less a mirror image of one other. But it turns out that symmetry is more than

Da Vinci's Vitruvian Man shows the symmetry of the human body. Da Vinci wanted to capture the ideal proportions and felt the human body was a microcosm (a small-scale representation) of the universe.

just a Renaissance ideal of beauty. Modern scientists have found that symmetry offers many advantages. Even when the differences are tiny, the most symmetrical people tend to be faster and healthier than their more irregular counterparts. They're also considered more attractive—and they even smell better!

NICE GENES

But building a truly symmetrical body (where the mirror images are a perfect match) is harder than it looks. To get symmetry right, your body needs to be good at a wide variety of tasks, like absorbing nutrients, distributing energy evenly, and forming proteins. In that sense, symmetry can act as a kind of "health certificate," showing that your internal systems are working well, and you had a normal, healthy development, says evolutionary biologist John Manning of Northumbria University, Newcastle upon Tyne, in the United Kingdom.

Instead of looking at just one body part, researchers measure the symmetry of ten or twelve different points in the body—such as the length of the index fingers, the widths of the wrists, ankles and knees, the size of the feet, and more. They add up all the measurements to check how symmetrical a person is as a whole.

"None of us actually achieve perfect symmetry on all our traits," Manning says. But some people get very close, with only tiny differences between the left and right sides of their body. These very symmetrical people are less likely to have health problems, are less prone to depression, and even tend to have a higher IQ. A recent study that measured the handgrip strength of sixty-nine men found that the more symmetrical men were also stronger.

Usain Bolt is a Jamaican sprinter. He is known as the fastest man alive. A study of competitive sprinters in Jamaica revealed that the athletes with the most perfectly symmetrical knees were the fastest.

Many of these benefits aren't caused by the symmetry itself. Instead, overall symmetry is probably a sign that someone is healthy and has good genes. But in some cases, being particularly symmetrical can help a body perform better.

That seems to be the case with runners. Evolutionary biologist Robert Trivers of Rutgers University in New Jersey studied competitive sprinters in Jamaica, and compared their measurements to average Jamaican bodies. Trivers used calipers to measure the width of each knee at its widest point. He looked for runners whose left knee was almost exactly the same width as the right. "The elite sprinters had more symmetrical knees and ankles than normal people, but their feet were the same," he says. Among the athletes, the men and women with the most perfectly symmetrical knees were the best of the best.

In an earlier study, Trivers even found that symmetry could be used to predict future running ability. He measured the knees of 288 Jamaican children in 1996, and again in 2006. When he returned in 2010, he also measured their sprinting speed. "If you had more symmetrical knees when you were 8 years old, then 14 years later, when you were 22, you ran the 100-meter dash more quickly than less symmetrical individuals," he says.

ATTRACTIVE PROPORTIONS

While scientists might use sensitive instruments to measure whether a person is symmetrical, most of us can tell with a quick glance. That doesn't mean we're on the lookout for symmetry, just that we register the other person's face as attractive or unattractive, says Randy Thornhill, an evolutionary biologist at the University of New Mexico.

Early studies had people look at photos of members of the opposite sex and rate their attractiveness. Researchers found that people with more symmetrical faces were rated as being more attractive. Later, researchers used computers to alter the photographs, making the same face appear more or less symmetrical. They found that increasing the symmetry of the face made it even more attractive to the opposite sex.

It's not surprising that people tend to reach the peak of their symmetry at around nineteen or twenty years of age, Manning says. That's an age at which people tend to be dating or looking for a romantic partner. Why do we find symmetry so attractive? Part of the reason is because we're probably interested in finding someone who's healthy and has good genes.

People often are drawn to appealing features, which includes facial symmetry. Symmetry peaks in early adulthood, when many people are searching for romance.

But symmetry isn't just a sign of good health; it can also be an indicator of another important quality in a mate: fertility.

Humans aren't the only creatures who find symmetry a desirable quality. Much of Thornhill's early symmetry research was on scorpion flies. He found that male scorpion flies that had more symmetrical wings and other body parts were not only more successful in winning fights for food and resources, but female flies also preferred them as mates.

What's next for symmetry research? Trivers' Jamaican study is one of the most important projects now underway, Manning says, because it's followed the same group of people for almost twenty years, giving scientists a rare look at how human symmetry relates to health and fitness over time.

Scorpion flies proved to be valuable subjects for research on symmetry. Can you see the symmetry in this scorpion fly's wings? Even the spots on the wings are symmetrical.

Until now, most research has looked at the benefits of being born especially symmetrical. But Trivers says he next wants to study whether physical exercise and training can actually help people become more symmetrical. He plans to study the same group of Jamaican athletes as they work at becoming faster, measuring their knees at regular intervals. "We're planning to do more work to find out if knees get more symmetrical during this period of intense training," he says.

CHAPTER 3

UNIQUELY IDENTICAL

Do you know someone who is a twin? What do you think it's like to be a twin? Have you ever wished you had a twin to blame for those times you got in trouble? Or a twin to share your secrets with? Even though twins can be very similar, even identical, your twin is not another you.

There are two main types of twins: fraternal and identical. Fraternal (dizygotic, or two-egg) twins develop from two separate eggs that are fertilized at, or near, the same time. Fraternal twins are just like regular brothers and sisters who happen to be the same age.

Identical (monozygotic, or one-egg) twins happen when one fertilized egg splits in half, making two separate cell clusters.

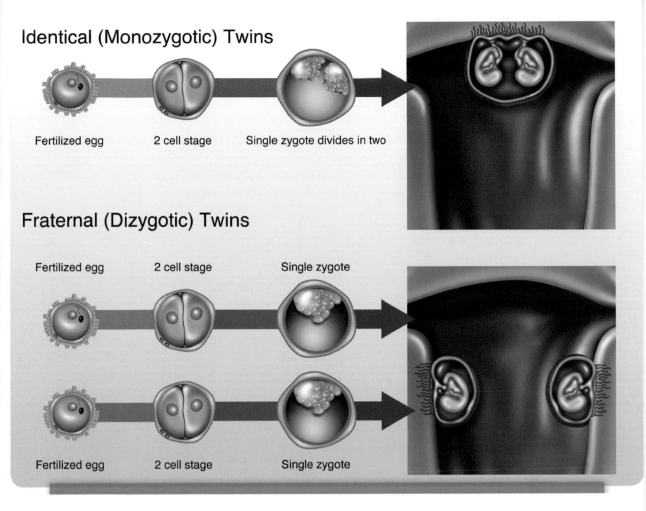

Identical (Monozygotic) Twins

Fertilized egg   2 cell stage   Single zygote divides in two

Fraternal (Dizygotic) Twins

Fertilized egg   2 cell stage   Single zygote

Fertilized egg   2 cell stage   Single zygote

This diagram shows the difference between twins that come from the same egg (identical) and twins that are in the uterus in two separate eggs (fraternal).

Because they originally came from the same fertilized egg, these babies share the same genetic plan. Identical twins look like, walk like, talk like, and sometimes think like each other—their brain-wave patterns can be similar. About 25 percent of identical twins will even "mirror" each other. For instance, one twin will be right-handed and the other will be left-handed.

The British Broadcasting Corporation (BBC) News reported last March that scientists have recently discovered a very unusual

These identical twin sisters look the same because they have the same DNA. However, while their genes are identical, their fingerprints will still be different.

new type of twin called "semi-identical." According to Vivienne Souter, a geneticist at Banner Good Samaritan Medical Center in Phoenix, Arizona, "their similarity is somewhere between identical and fraternal twins." The genes of these twins are exactly the same, except for a small portion. It's difficult to tell for sure, but scientists think a single egg was fertilized by two sperm, and then the fertilized egg split. This means that each new cluster would have exactly the same genes from the mother, but different genes from the father.

DNA provides the genetic plan for how we look and who we are. Scientists have mapped DNA patterns for things like IQ, alcohol and smoking addictions, diseases, relationships, jobs, hobbies, fears, and even favorite foods. There are millions of differences in every person's DNA pattern, unless you're talking about identical twins.

Even identical twins raised apart tend to be similar in more than just appearance. They may prefer the same foods, have similar jobs, or even choose the same hairstyles.

But identical twins are never exactly alike. Their fingerprints and iris patterns will be different. Scientists study identical twins to find out more about all of us. How much of our behavior comes from our genes? How much from our life experiences? Whether you're talking about fraternal, identical, or semi-identical, twins are interesting, unique people—times two!

CHAPTER 4

THE TELLTALE TAILS OF TELOMERES

Do you have a scrapbook of family pictures? If you do, get it out and look at the people in it. Do they look the same now as they did a year ago? What about five years ago? Look at baby pictures of yourself (if you can bear it). In what obvious ways have you changed? The fact is, you've aged, and so have all the other people in your photo album. Aging isn't gray hair, sagging jowls, or stiff joints. It's a process that occurs in every cell of every person every minute of every day.

It's easy to tell who is younger and who is older in this photograph, but even the little boy is aging. His cells are changing all the time.

"It is never too soon to think about aging, because, truly, aging begins at conception," says Joanne Singleton, codirector of the Institute for Healthy Aging at Pace University in Brooklyn. "Anti-aging research focuses on many things. Some is directed to the future, and some focuses on the here and now." The "here and now" of Singleton's work promotes what she calls "healthy aging": not smoking, good nutrition, exercise for body and mind, maintenance of a positive attitude, and establishing good family relationships and social support.

The future of research on aging, on the other hand, looks not outward but inward, deep into the individual cells that make up the human body. If we kept photographs of our cells, we would see that they change over time as surely as our faces and bodies do.

GENES AND TELOMERES

Just as our outward appearance changes, so do our genes. Genes are the bits of DNA in the nucleus of a cell that control everything the cell does. The structures of genes change as we get older. One way

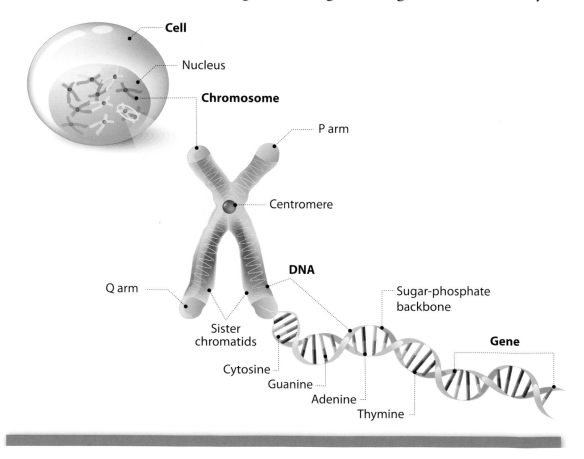

This diagram shows genes carried on the DNA. That DNA makes up each chromosome in a cell's nucleus.

they change is point mutations. These are changes in the order and arrangement of the single bases in DNA. Mutations happen because of exposure to chemicals in the environment, radiation from the sun, or sometimes just by chance. Experts estimate that each cell repairs between thirty thousand and seventy thousand DNA "damage events" every day.

Another change is in the function of genes, or gene expression. Much of the research on aging attempts to understand this process. As time passes, genes change how they operate, or whether they operate at all. At certain times, some genes switch on, while others switch off. Genes may function more or less efficiently at different times, or they may interact with other genes in new ways.

One factor that appears to be a major controller of gene expression is the telomere. Telomeres are long pieces of DNA at the ends of chromosomes. (Chromosomes are the structures in the nucleus of the cell that contain the genes.) Telomeres act like the plastic tips on the ends of shoelaces, says Texas A&M scientist Dorothy Shippen. "The integrity of the shoelace is maintained in large part because of this plastic tip," she says. "In the same way, the telomere provides the stability for the chromosomes through many divisions of the cell."

However, because of the way DNA copies itself, the chromosome loses a small piece of its telomere every time a cell divides. If we kept family albums of cell pictures, we'd see that telomeres shorten a little with each cell division. Eventually, they become so short that the cell can no longer divide. In that way, telomeres act as counters in the cell. They limit the number of cell divisions to between sixty and one hundred in a lifetime. This restricted number of divisions is called the "Hayflick Limit," named for Leonard Hayflick, who carried out research at the Wistar Institute in Philadelphia that led to the discovery. Limiting the number of cell divisions is a good thing, says University of Texas scientist Woodring E. Wright, because it acts as a natural barrier against cancer. Telomere shortening makes sure that cells don't divide too many times.

The cost of this natural protection, however, is aging. Like a shoelace that loses its tip, the end of the chromosome becomes "frayed." That triggers changes in gene expression throughout the cell. The cell changes its functions, growing a little less efficient with each shortening of a telomere. "This leads to either failure of the cell's structure and function or cellular death," Singleton says.

TELOMERASE

Many researchers think that slowing or stopping the shortening of telomeres might also slow or stop the aging process. Much of their research focuses on an enzyme called telomerase, which protects telomere length. The enzyme is naturally present in the body at certain times and in certain tissues. It's at work in the early embryo, but turned off in the fetus well before birth. It continues to operate, however, in certain cells in the digestive system, skin, and bone marrow. "The level of telomerase those cells express is sufficient to slow but not prevent telomere shortening," Wright explains. There's no proof that telomere shortening causes aging, but "we have good theoretical reasons to believe that it does," he says.

One such piece of evidence comes from studies of families with the rare, genetic disease dyskeratosis congenita. People with this disease inherit a defect in the telomerase enzyme. They have half the normal level of telomerase activity, and they have prematurely short telomeres. They also show signs of early, accelerated aging, including prematurely gray hair, spotty skin, slow healing of wounds, and increased risk of many diseases. "Since the only known function of telomerase is to maintain telomeres, this disease is the strongest evidence that loss of telomere maintenance is a cause, not just a sign, of at least some of the common aging-related traits and diseases," says geneticist Richard Cawthon at the University of Utah.

So, Cawthon thinks that increasing telomerase activity in cells might slow or stop aging. Whether that could work in healthy people is anybody's guess right now, but fighting disease with telomerase-affecting drugs is further along in showing success. One

This diagram shows telomerase elongating the telomere. If telomere shortening causes aging, then one can theorize that lengthening telomeres could slow or stop aging and age-related diseases.

TELOMERASE

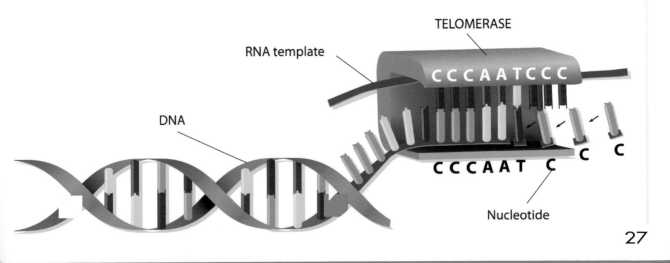

example comes from research on AIDS, the deadly disease caused by HIV (human immunodeficiency virus). As AIDS progresses, the telomeres of immune cells that normally attack and destroy HIV-infected cells get shorter. The immune cells die, allowing HIV to multiply and spread. The Geron Corporation in Menlo Park, California, has developed a drug that activates telomerase in immune cells. In tissue culture experiments, the drug dramatically slows telomere shortening. This might keep immune cells on the job fighting HIV longer. If the drug can pass its safety tests, it might be offered to AIDS patients someday.

Whether telomerase might safely be reactivated in healthy body cells to slow normal aging remains to be seen. "I think that telomeres are a big 'wait and see,' and that there will have to be a great deal more research that can then tie this to the overall aging equation," Singleton says.

In the meantime, we continue to add pictures to our photo albums. The pictures show us and our cells growing a little older every day.

TELOMERES AND CANCER

Cancer is cell division out of control. In 85 percent of cancer cells, telomerase activity is high. The enzyme prevents telomeres from shortening in cancer cells, so the cells become immortal. They never stop dividing, and they never die.

In May 2005, the Geron Corporation in Menlo Park, received permission from the US Food and Drug Administration to start clinical trials of a telomerase inhibitor drug. The drug, called GRN163L, blocks telomerase action. This allows telomeres to

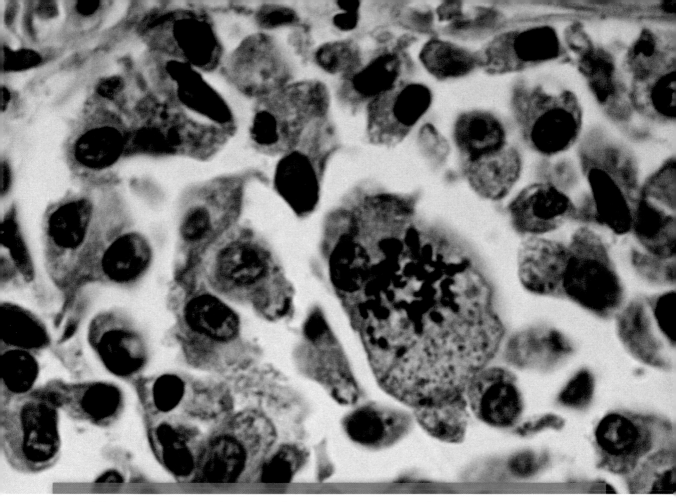

This image shows a close-up of a cancerous tumor in the connective tissue. Developing drugs that inhibit telomerase and allow telomeres to shorten could result in effective cancer treatment and perhaps, someday, even a cure.

shorten, cell division to stop, and (it is hoped) cancer cells to die. Nearly ten thousand people who had the most common form of leukemia tried the drug. The results were promising, although GRN163L has yet to approved for marketing. If it is, it may prove yet another way that research on telomeres can yield more years of healthy life for more people

CHAPTER 5

HUMAN LIFE SPAN: WHAT ARE THE LIMITS?

How old is old? Eighty? Ninety? One hundred, for sure. As the human life span increases, we need to adjust our thinking.

In early human history, a person would have been lucky to survive to age thirty. Now, the average American can expect to live into their late seventies. Most biodemographers—experts who analyze statistical information about populations—think that human life span has the potential to increase even further in the coming century. Just how far will it go? No one knows for sure, and there is a wide range of thought concerning the probable limit.

LIFE EVERLASTING?

One theory is that the human body has the potential to live hundreds and possibly thousands of years, although it would need quite a bit of help to do so. Dr. Aubrey de Grey, a computer scientist at the University of Cambridge in England and the main proponent of this theory, considers the human body to be like a machine that can undergo periodic maintenance and upgrading to keep it running in tip-top shape. If de Grey is correct, then as soon as it is technically possible, humans could dramatically lengthen their lives by an inestimable amount.

UP AND UP AND UP AND. . .

For most biodemographers, de Grey's ideas are a bit extreme and certainly not within the realm of possibility today. Even so, some of these researchers see the potential for human lives to reach one hundredand beyond.

Dr. James Vaupel, director of the Max Planck Institute for Demographic Research in Germany, is one such biodemographer. In 2002, Vaupel published a report in which he used census data collected periodically since 1840 to show that the average age at death has increased in a straight line right up to the present. Extrapolation of that line gave an estimated average life span of ninety years by the year 2050.

Vaupel argues that it is reasonable to expect the future to match the past—the line should keep moving upward as it has for the past 175 years. He explains that in the past, society found ways to improve the human condition and lives were extended. Therefore, he sees no reason to assume that such progress will stop.

Nowadays people are living longer than ever. Advances in medicine, better nutrition, and many other factors have contributed to this change.

OTHER FACTORS MUST BE CONSIDERED

Not all biodemographers agree with Vaupel. Dr. S. Jay Olshansky, professor of epidemiology and biostatistics at the University of Illinois at Chicago, finds flaws in simply extrapolating the observed trend. He explains that the trend reflects increases in life span brought about by improvements in fighting diseases during the early and mid-1900s. Because this prevented a lot of infants and children from dying (a real problem a hundred years ago), the number of people living long lives dramatically increased.

"But we can only save the young once," he says. "Now, we have to extend the lives of the old in order to make any further significant increases in the average life span." While he is optimistic that aging research will allow us to make advances in slowing the aging process, Olshansky does not think that the rate of change will be linear. He notes that the upward trend in average life expectancy gets much harder to increase as more and more of the population actually achieves the prize of having lived into their seventies.

In addition, Olshansky cautions that there is one factor that he sees as "an ominous storm approaching." The rise of childhood obesity seriously threatens to create a downturn in life span in the future, according to his research. Presently, one in five children and young adults between the ages of six and nineteen are obese. And obese children are more likely than their average weight peers to be obese as adults. He is quite concerned that unless we prevent the negative effects on health that accompany obesity, such as asthma, type 2 diabetes, heart disease, cancer, and depression, we could see life expectancy actually decrease several decades from now.

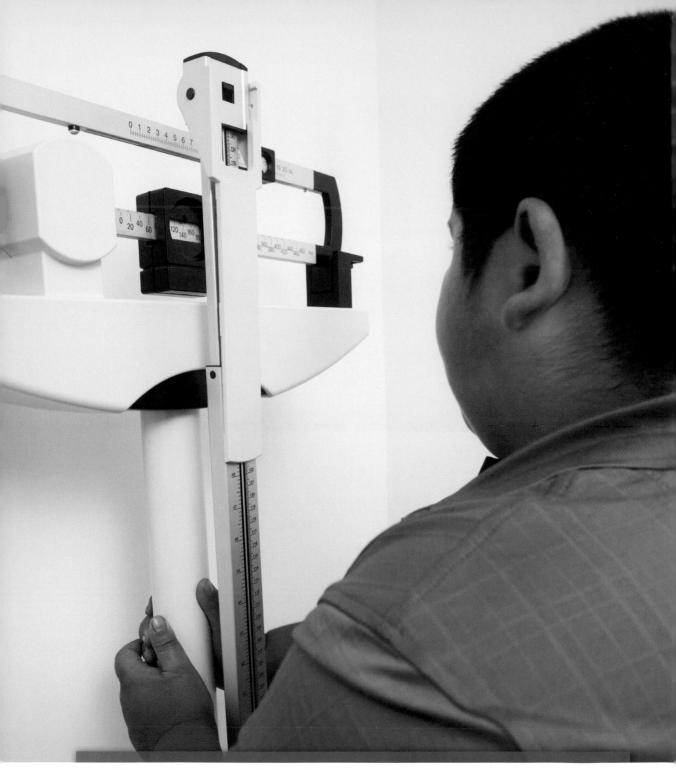

The number of obese children has risen significantly in recent years. Many schools are introducing programs to help children focus on exercise and healthy eating habits.

Jeanne Calment is photographed here at age 113. She lived to be 122 years old, making her the longest-lived person to have ever been documented.

THE FUTURE

So, what does the future hold for human life? Who knows? Certainly we can expect medical and technological improvements that will extend lives. We can also expect to see scientific progress in understanding aging, accompanied by new ways to slow it down.

However, many uncertainties also lie ahead. As we are seeing with obesity, there are health issues that can destroy the gains we have made in extending life span. Those uncertainties are at the heart of our inability to predict life span much more than a couple of years down the road. Whatever happens, though, it will be interesting!

CHAPTER 6

MIND VS. TIME: WHAT'S AHEAD FOR THE AGING BRAIN?

an you imagine yourself as an elderly person? Do you picture yourself wearing bifocals or using a cane? Would you be a hip and happening 180-year-old? Or would you have trouble remembering your own name? Genetics and environment determine how well or badly you age, but maybe one day science will override these factors.

THINKING YOUNG

Dr. Aubrey de Grey and various other scientists argue that science and technology can eventually conquer the problems of aging. Would the mind benefit from such a fountain of youth, too?

"I can't tell you that it's 'certain' that mental processes will be just as thoroughly maintained as physical ones," says de Grey, "because we don't know enough about how the brain works. But we certainly have good reason to be optimistic about that." After all, "the brain is made of cells just like the rest of our bodies, and the cells are made of the same sorts of molecules as our other cells."

Some of the "seven deadly things" that de Grey links to aging, indeed, factor into problems of the aging brain. For example, "extracellular junk" builds up in the brains of Alzheimer's disease (AD) patients. AD is the most common cause of dementia, according to the Alzheimer's Association. Almost 4.5 million Americans may have the progressive disease, including nearly half of people over age eighty-five. As AD progresses, clumps (called amyloid plaques) and tangles of fibers impair the brain's normal functions.

Cell damage also causes aging problems. Bruce Yankner and colleagues at Harvard Medical School (Cambridge, Massachusetts) recently studied preserved brains from people who had died at various ages up to 106. While there was significant variation, genes important for learning and memory were damaged in most older brains. While some people may compensate with no major loss in function, others may suffer serious loss of memory.

Yankner thinks that oxygen free radicals are the likely culprits behind such genetic damage. Free radicals are potentially toxic by-products produced when the body uses oxygen for energy. "However,

Healthy Brain

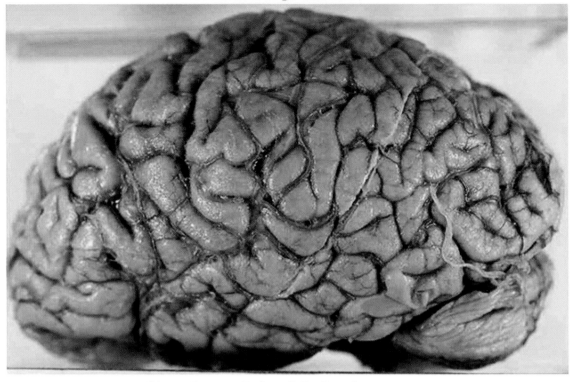

Brain with Alzheimer's

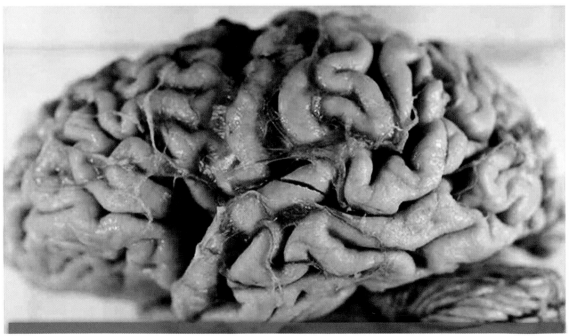

Here, a healthy brain (*top*) is compared to a brain affected by Alzheimer's disease (*bottom*). Notice the extensive loss of brain tissue, which affects memory, thinking, and behavior.

Dr. Bruce Yankner (*center*) speaks with two of his coauthors of a published study that discusses the effect of a certain protein, called REST, on Alzheimer's disease.

as we grow older, our ability to dispose of these free radicals declines," notes Yankner, "and they can then cause damage to our genes. This damage occurs when the free radical molecule combines with our DNA to change its structure."

ENGINEERING SOLUTIONS

Identifying what happens in the aging brain is a first step. But engineering ways to slow aging would require major leaps. Scientists are still studying many factors that affect cells and genetic activity. And they still don't know many things about how the mind works or what it can do.

Entropy, or increasing disorder, is another problem, says Preston Estep III, president and CEO of the biotechnology company Logenity, Inc. Think of how exchanges of increasingly corrupted information would eventually paralyze the Internet. Similarly, aging brings increasing disorder in how cells communicate in the brain and body.

Perhaps the biggest challenge in significantly extending life, says Estep, would be in "replacing or repairing parts of the brain without causing significant loss of memories or the person's identity." Nonetheless, he adds, "I think it is the destiny of humankind to continue to advance scientific knowledge to control disease and even aging."

IN THE MEANTIME. . .

We can't live for centuries yet, but we can still take steps to keep our brains sharp. Diets with foods rich in vitamins E and C may help. Those antioxidants may keep free radicals from damaging brain cells. Similarly, a "boot camp for the brain" at the UCLA Center on Aging features a low-fat diet with lots of fruits and vegetables, plus foods with omega-3 fatty acids, such as some fish and nuts.

Regular exercise tunes up your mind as well as your body. In recent studies, people who walked a couple of hours each week did better on memory and thinking tests and had lower risks of developing dementia than inactive people. Physical exercise improves cardiovascular health, which helps brain cells get adequate oxygen and nutrients.

Regular exercise also helps manage stress. When people feel overwhelmed, their ability to concentrate nosedives. Chronic stress also makes it easier for free radicals to damage DNA in cells and lower levels of telomerase, which, as you may recall, helps rebuild cells.

These foods are all rich in omega-3 fatty acids and fats
that are good for the brain and overall health.

Challenge and novelty are important, too, says Marian Diamond at the University of California, Berkeley. Rats in her lab lived longer when they had to climb over objects to get food, and when those objects changed often.

"Whatever you do, take it to the next step of complexity so that you are challenged," says Diamond. Simple examples include new or added responsibilities at home or school, puzzles or games, and sports. For novelty, keep finding new things to explore. Take different routes to school. Try different activities. In short, "Get out of a repetitive rut."

Staying active is an important key to overall good health for your brain and all your body systems. And, it can help slow the effects of aging.

Since rats in her lab lived longer when researchers held and petted them daily, Diamond adds tender, loving care to her list of ways to stay mentally vigorous. "Showing human beings you care for them never hurt anybody," as long as you do it appropriately, says Diamond. As the Roman poet Virgil (70–19 BCE) put it, "Love conquers all."

IMAGINING A WORLD OF IMMORTALS

While traditional geneticists and biologists are hoping to extend the human life span past age one hundred, one radical scientist is aiming to go much, much further. Believe it or not, he believes that one day, people could live long enough to celebrate their five thousandth birthdays!

No, this isn't science fiction. It's the remarkable prediction of Dr. Aubrey de Grey, the "maverick scientist" of anti-aging. While most researchers at work on the question of aging are doctors or biologists, de Grey is a computer expert. And, in fact, his solution to prevent aging sounds a lot like troubleshooting your computer!

De Grey believes that we can eliminate the effects of growing older by "fixing" seven key problems related to why cells grow old. According to de Grey, if we can fix these problems, people would stay young practically forever.

Some of the anti-aging techniques that de Grey has proposed are aimed at limiting mutations in mitochondria and chromosomes, similar to the goals being pursued by other experts. In fact, some of de Grey's other ideas about cell biology have proven to be true.

Still, most other experts in the field disagree with de Grey's predictions about "living forever." While he believes that aging can be "cured," they say that extending our life span by even a few years will require many years of effort. These experts say that, unlike a computer, the human body is far too complex to be "fixed" indefinitely in the way that de Grey describes. They worry that each "fix" could produce many problems of its own.

However, for right now, let's imagine that de Grey (or someone else) really could make a person live forever. What kind of world would that be?

Some people would predict that the world would become a much better place. For example, if people lived much longer, the next Einstein could work on important problems for hundreds of years—imagine how much knowledge he or she could acquire! Astronauts who lived for centuries would be able to travel to distant stars; they might even discover life in other solar systems. And if people lived much longer, perhaps we might become more responsible about war, pollution, or other problems that have long-term consequences.

Other people might predict that the world would become a very different place. For example, if people lived for centuries, would they still have children? If they did, how would we keep the planet from overcrowding? And if people never really aged, how old would they want to look? Would there be "youth" injections and "aging" injections? Would people lead just one life, or would they start over many times? What about "risky" behaviors, such as skydiving? Would they disappear—or be outlawed!?

Still other people might predict that the world would become a terrible place. For example, today, most exciting new ideas come from young people. But, if everyone lived much longer, maybe life would just stay the same and become a bore. Also, people from wealthy countries already live longer than people from poor ones. Would the same thing happen, if people could live much longer? What about wars and other rivalries? If people lived for centuries, would their hatreds and other negative behaviors also last forever?

Whatever the future holds, there is still a lot to learn about human growth and aging. For now, we can all eat healthy foods, exercise, and treat others as we want to be treated. If we do that, we might not only live longer, but we also might make the world a nicer one to live in!

GLOSSARY

cell The most basic structural and functional unit in a living organism.

chromosome A threadlike structure found in the nucleus, or center, of cells that carry genetic information.

dementia The deterioration of intellectual abilities such as concentration, memory, and judgment.

entropy Increasing disorder.

extrapolation Inference or estimation by extending or projecting known information.

gene A part of the DNA molecule that is the basis of heredity and passes on a certain characteristic from a parent to offspring.

genetics The study of heredity and inherited characteristics.

inherit To derive a quality, trait, or behavior from one's parents or ancestors through the genes.

mineral A solid, inorganic substance that occurs in nature.

mitochondria Little "power plants" in our cells that produce energy from glucose.

molecule The smallest particle that something can be divided into without changing its chemical properties; a group of atoms bonded together.

mutation A change the structure of a gene.

osteoblast A cell that makes the matter to create bones.

osteocyte A bone cell that is formed when the osteoblast becomes embedded in the matter it secretes, or puts out.

FURTHER READING

BOOKS

Kovacs, Vic. *Gene Therapy*. New York, NY: Gareth Stevens Publishing, 2017.

Mooney, Carla. *Genetics: Breaking the Code of Your DNA*. White River Junction, VT: Nomad Press, 2014.

Sjonger, Rebecca. *Biomedical Engineering and Human Body Systems*. New York, NY: Crabtree Publishing, 2015.

Thomspon, Tamara. *Extending the Human Lifespan*. Farmington Hills, MI: Greenhaven Press, 2013.

WEBSITES

Khan Academy, Developmental Biology
www.khanacademy.org/science/biology/developmental-biology
Learn how humans and other organisms develop from a single cell.

KidsHealth, What Are Wrinkles?
kidshealth.org/en/kids/wrinkles.html?ref=search
Read more about aging and why wrinkles form.

TeensHealth, The Basics on Genes and Genetic Disorders
kidshealth.org/en/teens/genes-genetic-disorders.html
Dive deeper into the world of genetics.

INDEX